Kee's Home

Kii Baghan Haz'ą́ągi

Kii Baghan Haz'ą́ą́gi

Kee's Home

A BEGINNING NAVAJO / ENGLISH READER by Geraldine Hall

With illustrations by Vera Louise Drysdale

Navajo translation by Irvy Goossen

NORTHLAND PRESS/FLAGSTAFF

FOURTH PRINTING, 1979

ISBN 0-87358-089-3

Library of Congress Catalog Card Number 72-174991

Composed and Printed in the United States of America

Foreword

RECENTLY A NUMBER OF TEACHERS on the reservation have discovered a renewed interest on the part of the Navajo people in learning to read their own language. In addition they have found that Navajo students, not only learn to read better in English, but are also more highly motivated to study English when they find that the marks on paper make sense in both languages.

Geraldine Hall, who has taught reading classes at all eight grade levels, has employed this knowledge in the concept and preparation of this bilingual primer. While the Navajo child is learning to read in his own language, he will be seeing the corresponding English word on the same page. This association at the beginning of the reading process should make the transition to reading in English an easier and much less awesome procedure.

As a teaching aid, I have prepared a glossary which introduces the

Navajo alphabet and fundamentals of pronunciation. Also included is a list of the seventy words introduced in the text — the English and its Navajo equivalent, which is written according to Navajo phonetics.

IRVY GOOSSEN

Introduction

THIS BOOK WAS DESIGNED to fill a great need for beginning Navajo readers. Almost 23,000 Navajo children are enrolled in Bureau of Indian Affairs schools. Of this number, more than 2,700 will be entering first grade this year, and proportionately more in subsequent years. Most of these children come to school with a limited background of experiences when compared to the average American child, and ninety per cent of them know little or no English. It is both unreasonable and unrealistic to expect them to learn to read in a language foreign to them when they have not learned to read in their own.

Kee's Home is a bilingual book — the Navajo words and their English equivalents appear on each page of the text. We selected only those English words which are completely translatable into Navajo without any change of meaning. Such a text was made possible with the help of Irvy Goossen, to whom I am grateful. For easy distinction, the

Navajo and English words are printed in different colors. Words and phrases are introduced gradually, the entire vocabulary is controlled, and repetitions are made where possible to give necessary practice.

Both text and illustrations are directed toward incidents and settings to which the Navajo child can relate, and are intended to create an interest in learning to read. It is hoped that through this approach, reading will become a happy and meaningful experience for Navajo children. For English speaking children, the book may also serve as a primer, in addition to providing a glimpse of Navajo life and an introduction to the Navajo language.

I wish to extend my sincere thanks to all those who have helped by their suggestions and encouragement. Special thanks to Vera Drysdale of Santa Fe for her beautiful illustrations, which add so much, and to my Navajo consultant, Loretta Begay of Many Farms.

GERALDINE HALL
Many Farms School

Kii éí yinishyé.

My name is Kee.

T'áá diné nishłį́.

I am Navajo.

Díí éí shilééchąą'í.

Shilééchąą'í Shep wolyé.

This is my dog.

My dog's name is Shep.

Hágo.

Hágo, shaa nínááh.

Hágo, Shep.

Come.

Come here.

Come, Shep.

Shep shich'į' yilwoł.

Hágo, Shep.

Shep is coming to me.

Come, Shep.

Shep! Shep!
Shilééchąą'í shił yá'át'ééh.

Shep! Shep!
I like my dog.

Kii dóó Shep.

Kee and Shep.

Shí naashnish.

Dibé dóó tł'ízí baa áháshyą́.

I work.

I take care of the sheep and goats.

Shilééchąą'í shíká análwo'.

Shilééchąą'í dibé dóó
tł'ízí yaa áhályą́.

My dog helps me.

My dog takes care
of the sheep and goats.

Díí éí shideezhí.

This is my sister.

Baa' wolyé.

Her name is Bah.

Baa' shíká análwo'.

Shideezhí shíká análwo'.

Neiilnish.

Bah is helping me.

My sister is helping me.

We are working.

Hágo, Shep.

Shíká anilyeed.

Hágo, kodi.

Come, Shep.

Help me.

Come here.

Da'dinishtįįh.

Baa' shíká iilyeed.

Dibé baa áhwiilyą́.

I close the gate.

Bah is helping me.

We take care of the sheep.

Díí Baa' bimósí.

This is Bah's cat.

Kii, shíká anilyeed.

Shimósí bíká anilyeed.

Kee, help me.

Help my cat.

Dooda, dooda!

Doo ál'įį da!

No, no!

Don't do that!

Díí éí shimósí.

Shimósí shił yá'át'ééh.

This is my cat.

I like my cat.

Díí éí shimá.

This is my mother.

Shimá bíká anáshwo'.

Chizh bá nináháshjááh.

Neiilnish.

I help my mother.

I help her with firewood.

We work.

Shimá naalnish.

Dah díníilghaazh íílééh.

My mother works.

She makes frybread.

Shilééchąą'í aadę́ę́' yilwoł.

Baa' bimósí ałdó' yilwoł.

Dichin nízin.

My dog is coming.

Bah's cat is coming.

They are hungry.

Shep éí dichin nízin.

Dah díníilghaazh ła' yinízin.

Dah díníilghaazh nihił łikan.

Shep is hungry.

He wants some frybread.

We like frybread.

Shilééchąą'í dah díníilghaazh yiyą́.

Baa' bimósí ałdó' dah díníilghaazh yiyą́.

Dah díníilghaazh éí łikan.

My dog eats frybread.

Bah's cat eats frybread.

Frybread is good.

Blacky éí shiłį́į́'.

Blacky is my horse.

Blacky, hágo.

Wóshdę́ę́', kodi.

Come, Blacky.

Come here.

Shilį́į́' shił yá'át'ééh.

Łį́į́' yá'át'éehii át'é.

I like my horse.

He is a good horse.

Blacky shíká análwo'.

Neiilnish.

Dibé dóó tł'ízí baa áhwiilyą́.

Blacky helps me.

We are working.

We take care of the sheep and goats.

Awéé' éí sitsilí yázhí.

The baby is my little brother.

Awéé'éí Baa' bitsilí yázhí.

The baby is Bah's little brother.

Aayá!

Sitsilí yázhí.

T'áadoo áńt'íní!

Ouch!

My little brother.

Don't do that!

Dibé naniilkaad doo.

Łį́į́' bee naniilkaad doo.

We will herd sheep.

We will herd them with horses.

Kwe'é shideezhí dóó sitsilí yázhí.

Here are my sister and little brother.

Díí éí shizhé'é.

This is my father.

Shizhé'é náádááł.

Naalnish ńt'éé'.

My father is coming home.

He was working.

Hágo, shideezhí!

Nihizhé'é náádááł.

Come, my sister!

Father is coming.

Shimá! Shimá!

Shizhé'é nádzá.

Mother! Mother!

My father is home.

Shimá dóó shizhé'é kwe'é.

My mother and father are here.

Díí éí shaghan.

This is my home.

Baa' dóó shí kwe'é nihighan.
Nihighan nihił yá'át'ééh.

Bah and I live here.
We like our home.

Wóshdę́ę́'.

Shimá dóó shizhé'é kwe'é baghan.

Shideezhí dóó sitsilí yázhí kwe'é baghan.

Come in.

My father and mother live here.

My sister and little brother live here.

Shimá naalnish.

Awéé' yaa áhályą́.

Sitsilí yázhí yaa áhályą́.

My mother works.

She takes care of the baby.

She takes care of my little brother.

Dooda, dooda, Blacky!

Ch'ínílyeed!

Nówehjį'!

No, no, Blacky!

Get out!

Go away!

Kwe'é naháatą.

Here we are.

Hooghan góne' naháatą́.

Da'iidą́.

Nihił dahózhǫ́.

We are in our home.

We are eating.

We are happy.

Kwe'é neii'né.

Neii'néego nihił yá'át'ééh.

Hooghangi nihił dahózhǫ́.

We are playing here.

We like to play.

We are happy in our home.

Glossary

VOWELS

1.   There are basically four vowels in the Navajo alphabet. The vowels are as follows, the first example being a Navajo word; the last, the closest approximation in an English word:

a	hágo	(come here!)	are
e	dibé	(sheep)	Shep
i	chizh	(firewood)	is
o	hágo	(come here!)	go

2.   Vowels may be either long or short in duration, the long vowels being indicated by a doubling of the letter. The length does not affect the quality of the vowel except that /ii/ is always pronounced as /i/ in machine.

i	haz'ą́ągi	(at a place)	is
ii	díí	(this, these)	deep

95

3. Vowels with hooks under them are nasalized. To nasalize, some of the breath passes through the nose in producing the sound.

a̧a̧	shiléécha̧a̧'í	(dog)
ę́ę́	wóshdę́ę́'	(this way!)
į́į́	łį́į́'	(horse)
ǫ́	nihił dahózhǫ́	(we are happy)

4. When there is a tone mark on a letter, raise your voice in pitch on that syllable.

dibé	di︱bé	(sheep)
nínááh	nínááh	(you come)
góne'	gó︱ne'	(inside)

5. Two diphthongs are used in this book: ei, eii. Both sound somewhat like ay as in hay. The first one is higher in tone; the second one lower and longer.

6. When only the first element of a vowel or a dipththong has a mark above it, the tone is falling.

doo ál'į da	(it isn't done)
dah díníilghaazh	(frybread)

7. The glottal stop /'/ is the most common consonantal sound in Navajo. It sounds like the break between "oh, oh." The breaks in *yá'át'ééh* are glottal stops.

8. Following are the rest of the consonants and their English equivalents, as nearly as they can be given.

b	Baa'	Bah — girl's name	like p in spot
ch	chizh	firewood	like ch in church
ch'	ch'íníyeed	run out	. . . .
d	dibé	sheep	like t in stop
dl	dlǫ́ǫ́'	prairie dog	like dl in paddling
dz	nádzá	he returned	like dz in adze
g	góne'	inside	like k in sky
gh	hooghan	hogan	. . . .
h	hágo	come here	. . . .
hw	hweeshne'	I told him	like wh in when
j	jádí	antelope	like j in jug
k	Kii	Kee — boy's name	like k in kitten
k'	k'ad	now	. . . .
kw	kwe'é	right here	like qu in quick
l	naalnish	he works	like l in lazy

97

ł	łį́į́'	horse	. . . .
m	mósí	cat	like m in man
na	naalnish	he works	like n in new
s	mósí	cat	like s in soon
sh	shí	I	like sh in shoe
t	naháatą	we sit	. . . .
t'	yá'át'ééh	it is good	. . . .
tł	tłah	ointment	. . . .
tł'	tł'ízí	goat	. . . .
ts	sitsilí	my younger brother	like ts in hats
ts'	ts'ah	sagebrush	. . . .
w	Wááshindoon	Washington, D. C.	like w in wash
y	yá	sky	like y in yes
z	zas	snow	like z in zero
zh	bizhé'é	his father	like z in azure

WORD LIST

Page numbers listed are those on which the word first appears.

PAGE	NAVAJO	ENGLISH
2	Kii	Kee - boy's name
2	éí	that, that one
2	yinishyé	I am called
4	t'áá diné	Navajo
4	nishłį	I am
6	díí	this
6	shilééchąą'í	my dog
6	Shep	Shep
6	wolyé..........	he is called
8	hágo	come! come here!
8	shaa	to me
8	nínááh	you are coming
10	shich'į'	to me
10	yilwoł	he runs
12	shił yá'át'ééh ...	I like it
14	dóó	and

PAGE	NAVAJO	ENGLISH
16	shí	I
16	naashnish	I am working
16	baa áháshyą . . .	I take care of them
18	dibé	sheep
18	tł'ízí	goat, goats
18	shíká análwo'. . . .	he helps me
18	yaa áhályą	he/she takes care of them
20	Baa' shideezhí . . .	Bah - girl's name
	. . . .	my younger sister
24	neiilnish.	we work
26	shíká anilyeed . . .	you help me
26	kodi	here
28	da'dinishtįįh	I close it (a gate)
28	shíká iilyeed	he/she helps me
28	baa áhwiilyą.	we take care of them
30	bimósí	her cat
32	shimósí	my cat
34	dooda	no
34	ál'į.	one does it

PAGE	NAVAJO		ENGLISH
50	shiłį́į́'	. . . .	my horse
52	wóshdę́ę́'	. . . .	this way!
54	łį́į́'	. . . .	horse
54	yá'át'éehii	. . . .	a good one
54	át'é	. . . .	it is
56	shíká análwo'	. . . .	he/she helps me repeatedly
58	sitsilí	. . . .	my younger brother
58	yázhí	. . . .	the little one
58	awéé'	. . . .	baby
60	bitsilí	. . . .	his/her younger brother
62	aayá!	. . . .	ouch!
62	t'áadoo ánt'íní	. . .	don't do it!
64	naniilkaad	. . . .	we herd them (sheep)
64	doo	. . . .	it will be (indicates future)
64	bee	. . . .	with, by means of it
66	kwe'é	. . . .	right here
68	shizhé'é	. . . .	my father
70	náádááł	. . . .	he is coming back
70	ńt'éé'	. . . .	it was (indicates past)